PIANO SOLO

BLENDED WORSHIP
PIANO COLLECTION

ISBN 978-1-5400-5132-5

Visit Hal Leonard Online at
www.halleonard.com

Contact us:
Hal Leonard
7777 West Bluemound Road
Milwaukee, WI 53213
Email: info@halleonard.com

In Europe, contact:
Hal Leonard Europe Limited
42 Wigmore Street
Marylebone, London, W1U 2RN
Email: info@halleonardeurope.com

In Australia, contact:
Hal Leonard Australia Pty. Ltd.
4 Lentara Court
Cheltenham, Victoria, 3192 Australia
Email: info@halleonard.com.au

CONTENTS

AMAZING GRACE
(My Chains Are Gone)

Words by JOHN NEWTON
Traditional American Melody
Additional Words and Music by CHRIS TOMLIN
and LOUIE GIGLIO

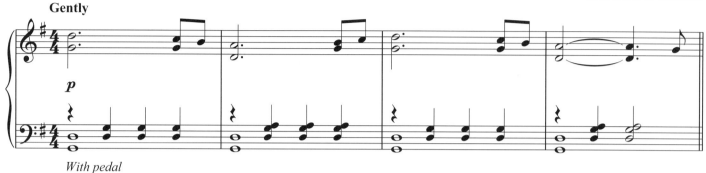

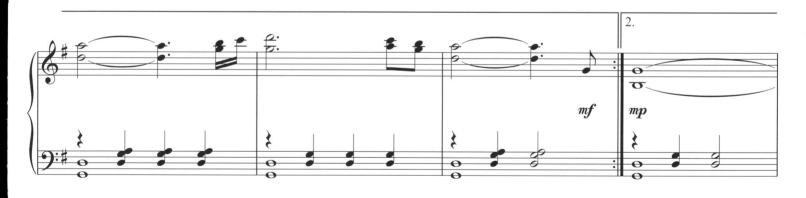

DRAW ME CLOSE

Words and Music by
KELLY CARPENTER

Moderately slow

With pedal

Bring out melody

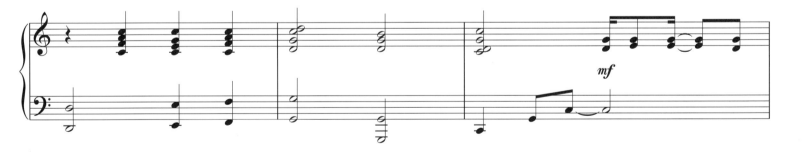

ANCIENT WORDS

Words and Music by
LYNN DeSHAZO

Moderately

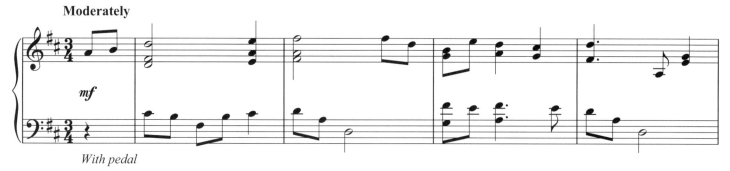

With pedal

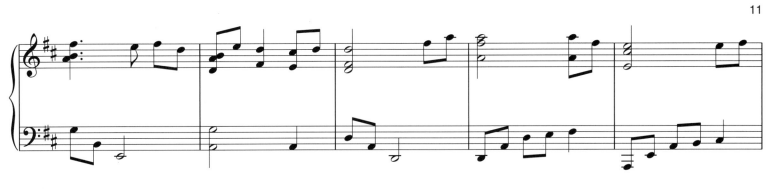

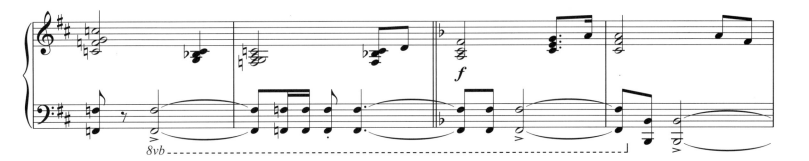

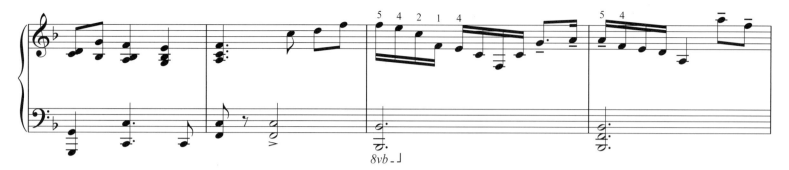

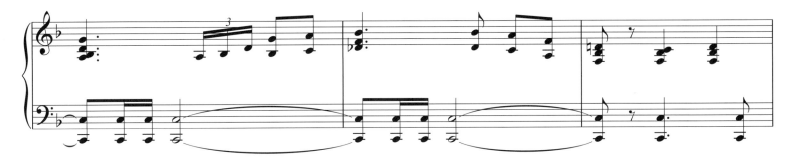

BE THOU MY VISION

Traditional Irish

cresc.

mf

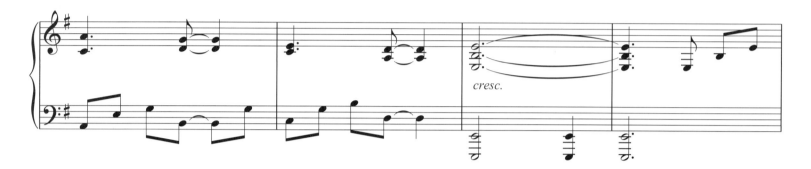

COME, CHRISTIANS, JOIN TO SING

Words by CHRISTIAN HENRY BATEMAN
Traditional Spanish Melody

molto rit.

COME THOU FOUNT, COME THOU KING

Traditional
Additional Words and Music by
THOMAS MILLER

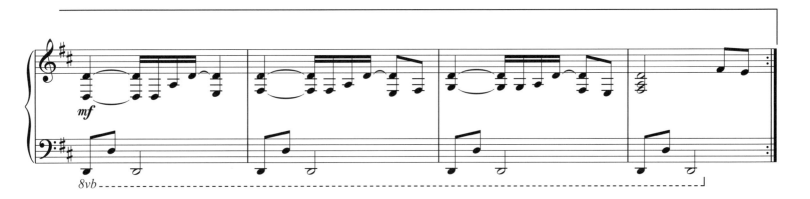

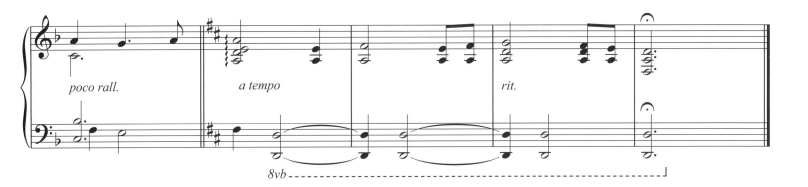

CORNERSTONE

Words and Music by JONAS MYRIN,
REUBEN MORGAN, ERIC LILJERO
and EDWARD MOTE

GIVE THANKS

Words and Music by
HENRY SMITH

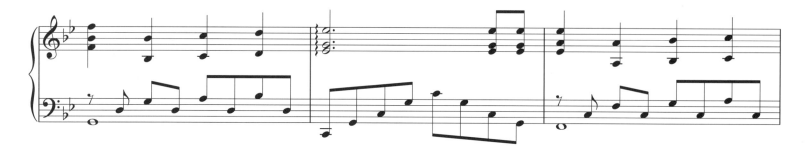

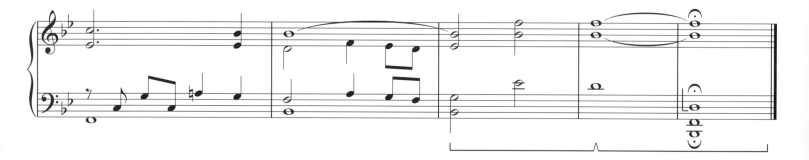

FAIREST LORD JESUS

Words from *Münster Gesangbuch*
Music from *Schlesische Volkslieder*

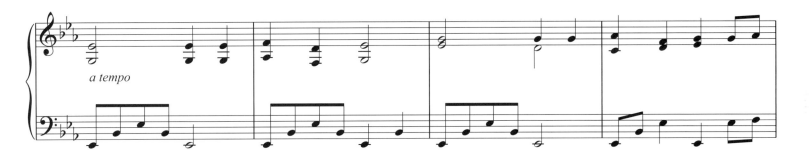

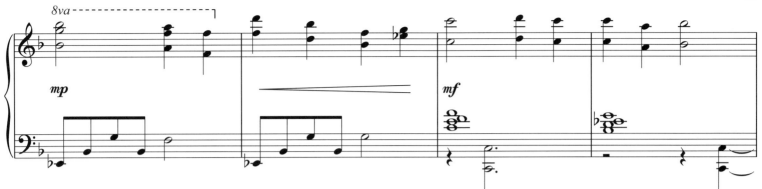

GREAT IS THY FAITHFULNESS

Words by THOMAS O. CHISHOLM
Music by WILLIAM M. RUNYAN

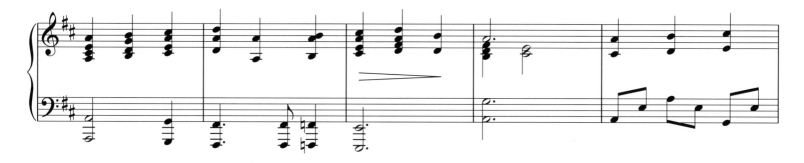

THE HEART OF WORSHIP
(When the Music Fades)

Words and Music by
MATT REDMAN

Steady Ballad

With pedal

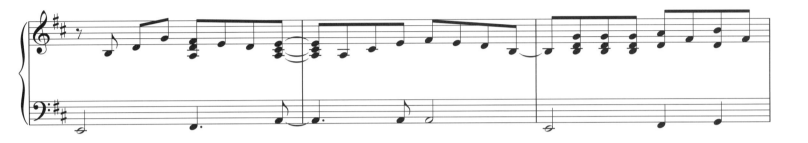

HE IS EXALTED

Words and Music by
TWILA PARIS

Flowing, not too fast

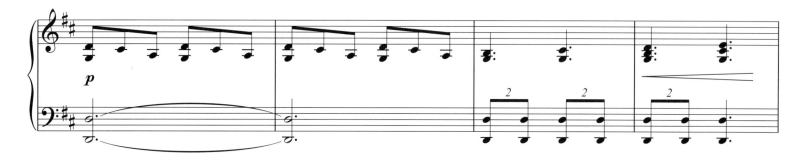

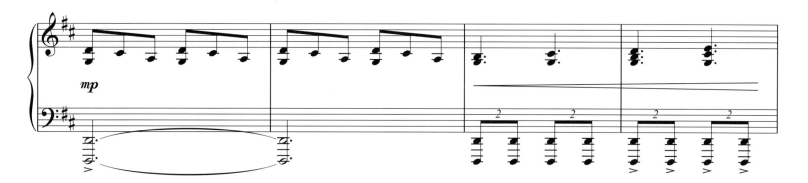

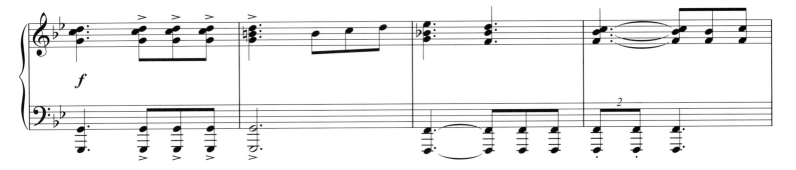

HERE I AM TO WORSHIP
(Light of the World)

Words and Music by
TIM HUGHES

Moderately slow

molto rit.

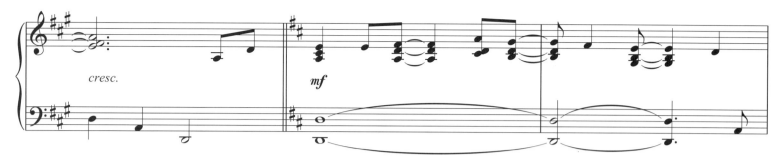

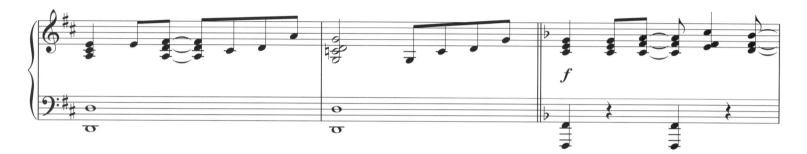

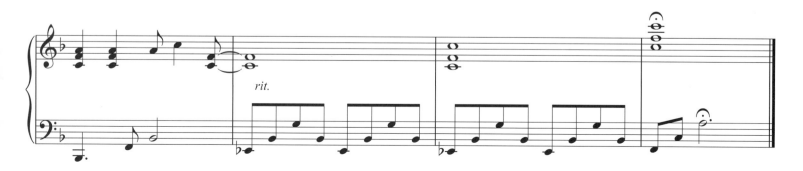

I WILL RISE

Words and Music by CHRIS TOMLIN,
JESSE REEVES, LOUIE GIGLIO
and MATT MAHER

Moderately

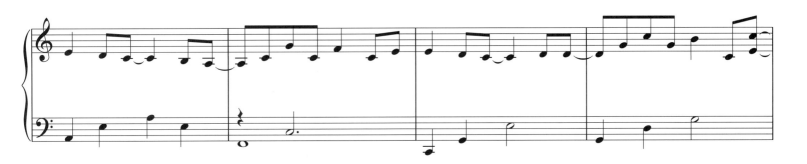

D.S. al Coda

CODA

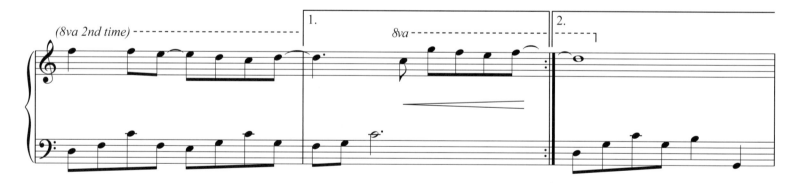

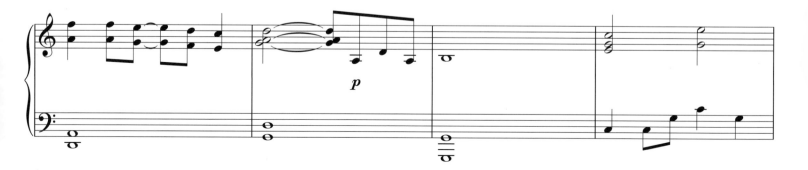

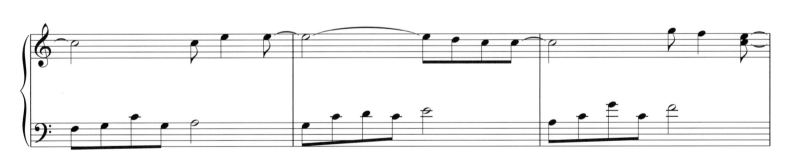

HOLY, HOLY, HOLY

Text by REGINALD HEBER
Music by JOHN B. DYKES

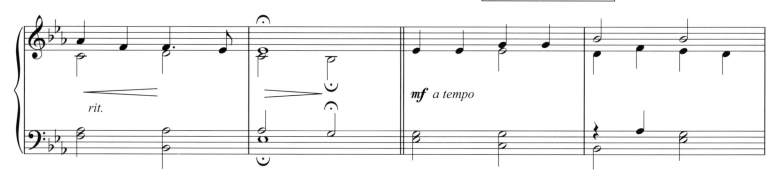

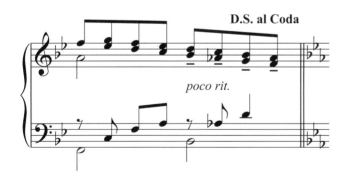

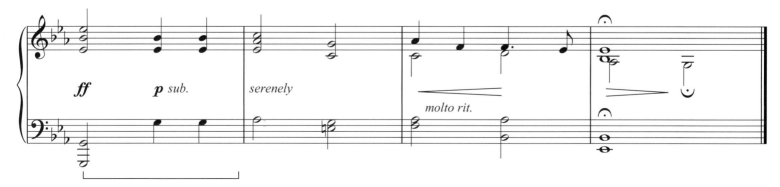

HOW DEEP THE FATHER'S LOVE FOR US

Words and Music by
STUART TOWNEND

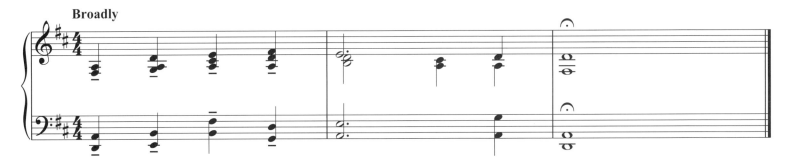

HOW GREAT IS OUR GOD

Words and Music by CHRIS TOMLIN,
JESSE REEVES and ED CASH

With praise

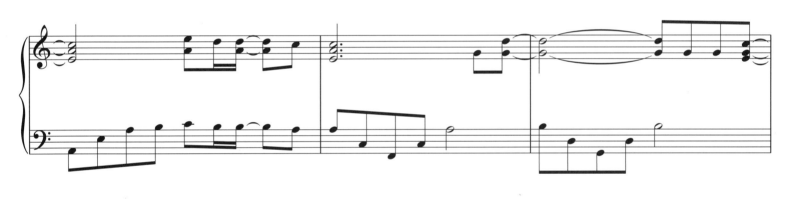

HOW GREAT THOU ART

Words by STUART K. HINE
Swedish Folk Melody Adapted
and Arranged by STUART K. HINE

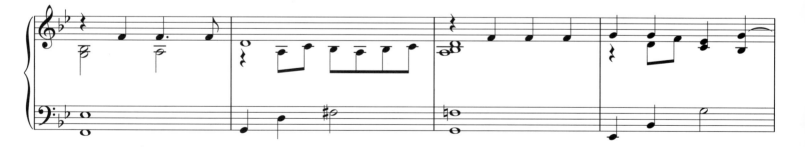

(bring out melody)

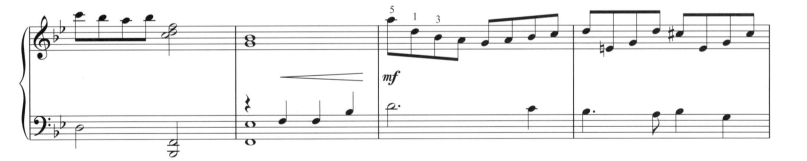

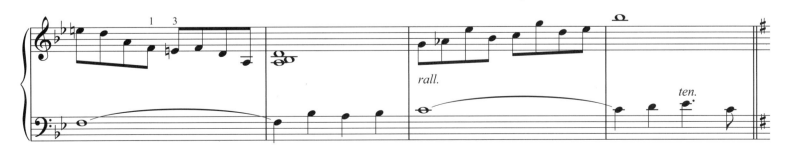

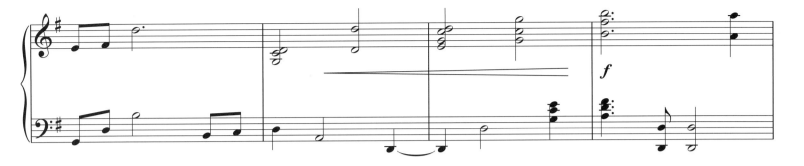

I GIVE YOU MY HEART

Words and Music by
REUBEN MORGAN

Worshipfully

JESUS MESSIAH

Words and Music by CHRIS TOMLIN,
JESSE REEVES, DANIEL CARSON
and ED CASH

With praise

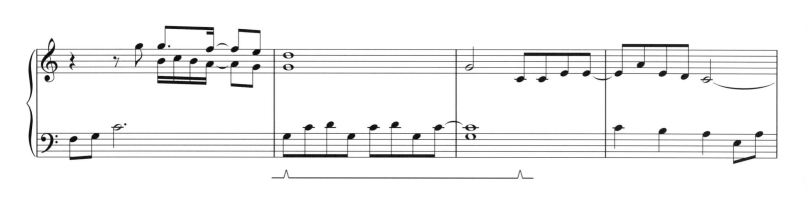

JOYFUL, JOYFUL, WE ADORE THEE

Words by HENRY VAN DYKE
Music by LUDWIG VAN BEETHOVEN,
melody from *Ninth Symphony*
Adapted by EDWARD HODGES

Brightly

LAMB OF GOD

Words and Music by
TWILA PARIS

Reflectively

p

With pedal

mp

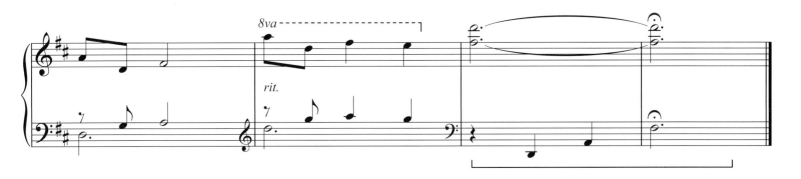

LORD, I LIFT YOUR NAME ON HIGH

Words and Music by
RICK FOUNDS

LEAD ME TO THE CROSS

Words and Music by
BROOKE LIGERTWOOD

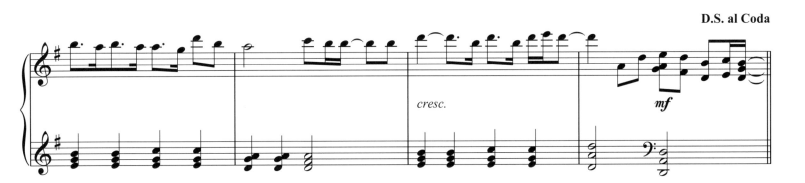

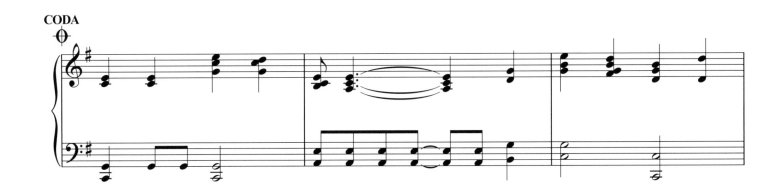

LORD, I NEED YOU

Words and Music by JESSE REEVES,
KRISTIAN STANFILL, MATT MAHER,
CHRISTY NOCKELS and DANIEL CARSON

Moderate Ballad

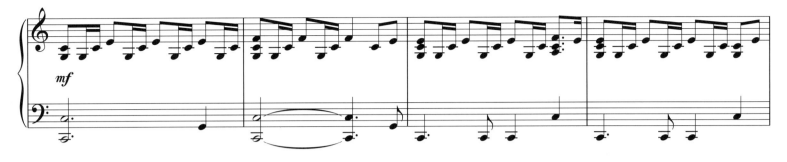

THE POWER OF THE CROSS
(Oh to See the Dawn)

Words and Music by STUART TOWNEND
and KEITH GETTY

Freely

Moderately slow

Broadly

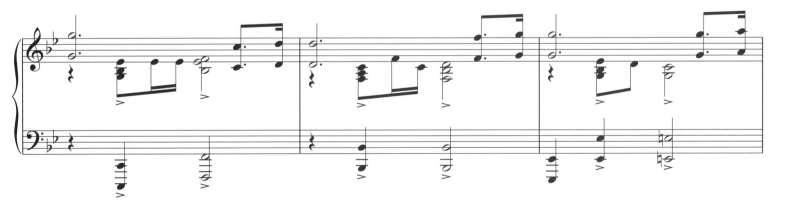

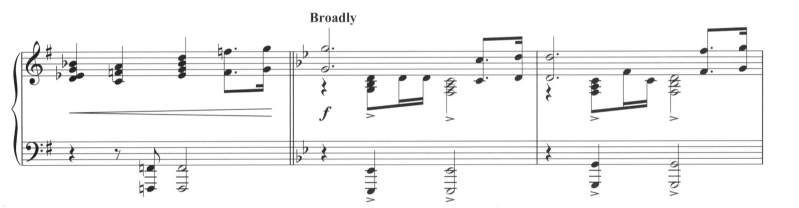

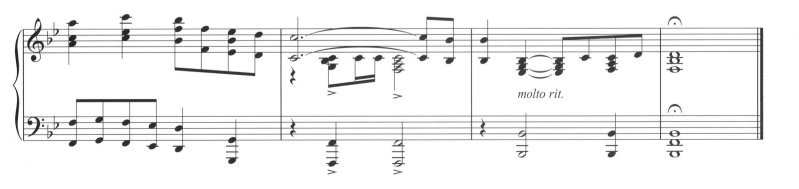

MAJESTY

Words and Music by
JACK HAYFORD

Stately, in 2

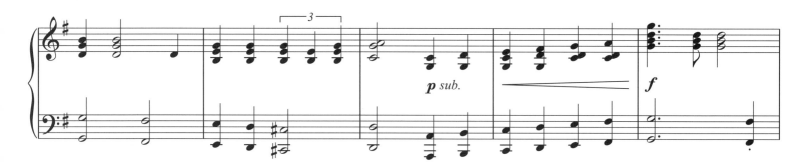

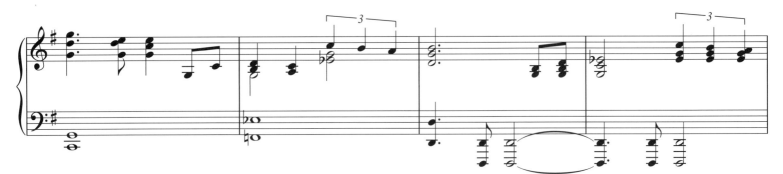

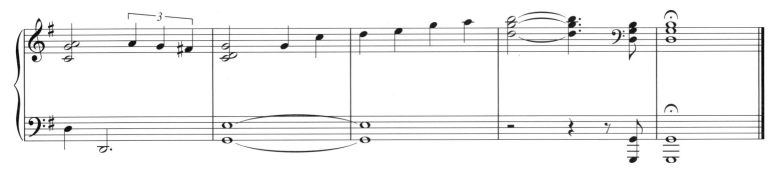

MIGHTY TO SAVE

Words and Music by BEN FIELDING
and REUBEN MORGAN

94

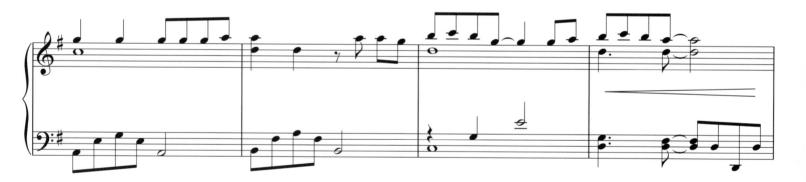

O CHURCH ARISE

Words and Music by KEITH GETTY
and STUART TOWNEND

Steadily

OPEN THE EYES OF MY HEART

Words and Music by
PAUL BALOCHE

With steady drive

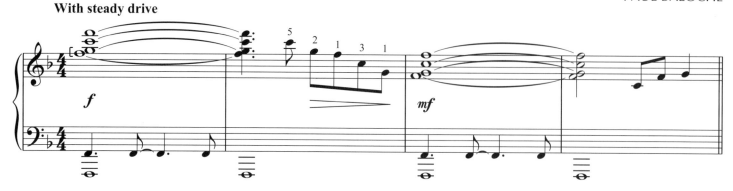

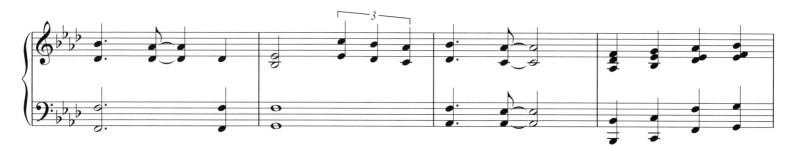

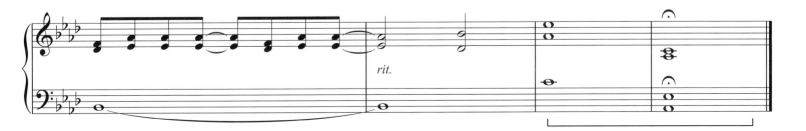

PRAISE TO THE LORD, THE ALMIGHTY

Words by JOACHIM NEANDER
Translated by CATHERINE WINKWORTH
Music from *Erneuerten Gesangbuch*

Joyfully

SHOUT TO THE LORD

Words and Music by
DARLENE ZSCHECH

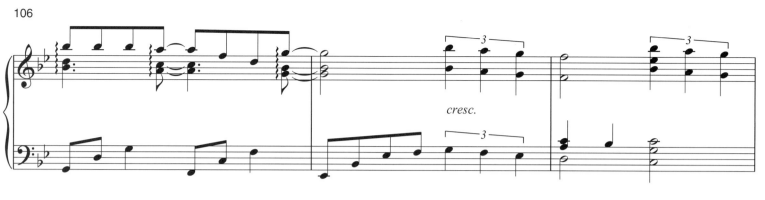

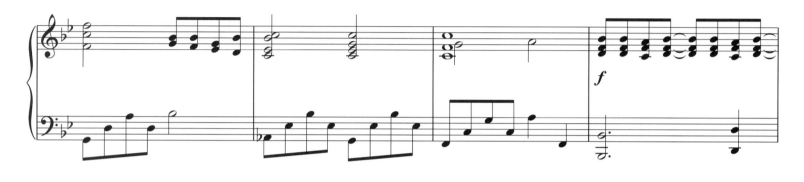

D.S. al Coda

CODA

SHINE, JESUS, SHINE

Words and Music by
GRAHAM KENDRICK

Moderately

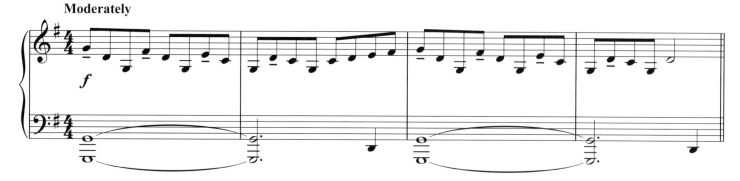

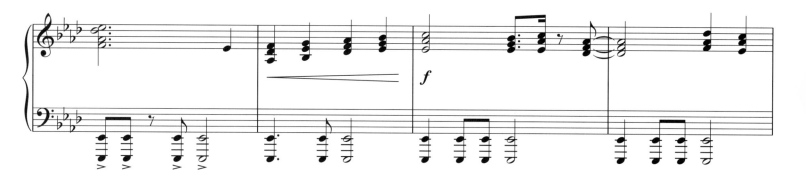

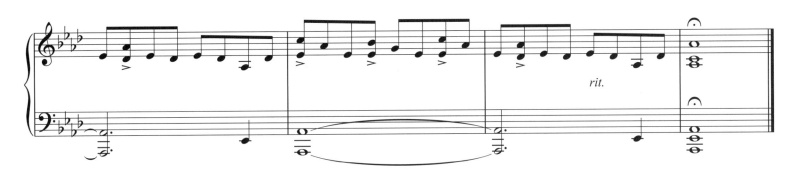

SHOUT TO THE NORTH

Words and Music by
MARTIN SMITH

Flowing, in 2

With pedal

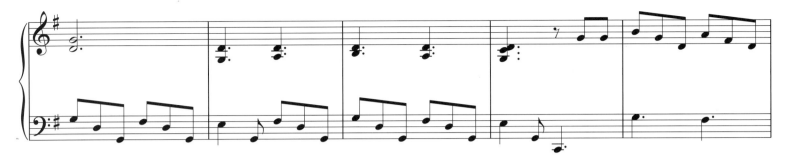

10,000 REASONS
(Bless the Lord)

Words and Music by JONAS MYRIN
and MATT REDMAN

Moderate Ballad

TAKE MY LIFE AND LET IT BE

Words by FRANCES R. HAVERGAL
Music by HENRY A. CÉSAR MALAN

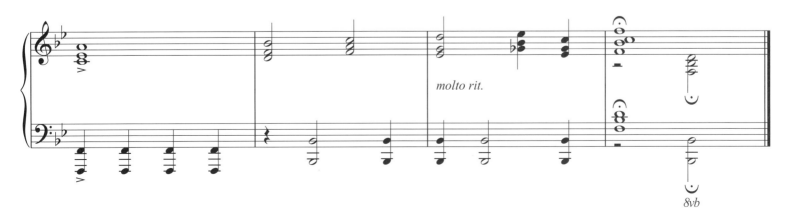

THERE IS A REDEEMER

Words and Music by
MELODY GREEN

YOUR NAME

Words and Music by PAUL BALOCHE
and GLENN PACKIAM

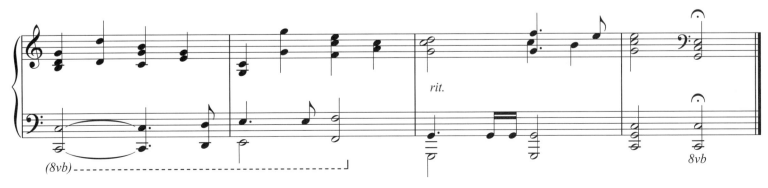

TO GOD BE THE GLORY

Words by FANNY J. CROSBY
Music by WILLIAM H. DOANE

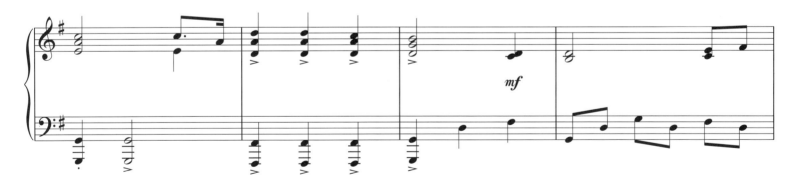

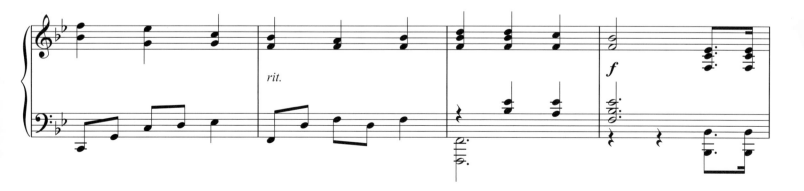

Regally, a little slower

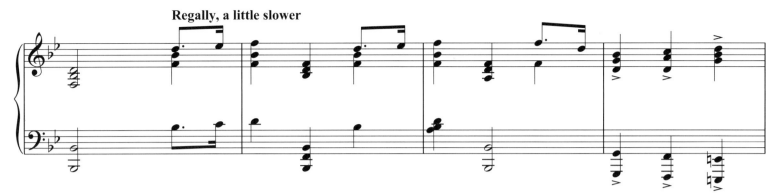

Broadly

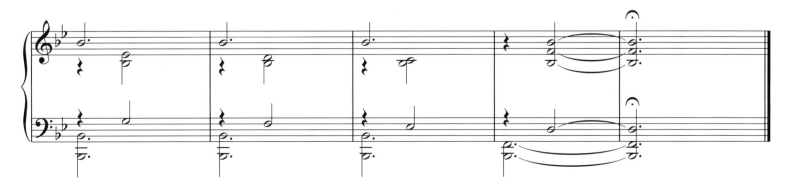

WORTHY IS THE LAMB

Words and Music by
DARLENE ZSCHECH

Worshipfully

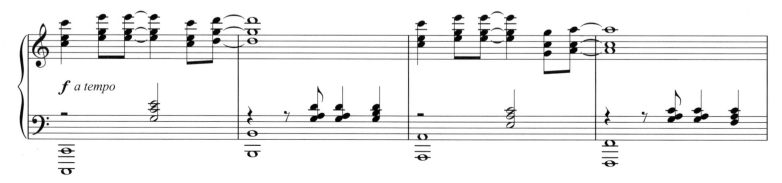

The Best
PRAISE & WORSHIP
Songbooks for Piano

Above All
THE PHILLIP KEVEREN SERIES
15 beautiful praise song piano solo arrangements by Phillip Keveren. Includes: Above All • Agnus Dei • Breathe • Draw Me Close • He Is Exalted • I Stand in Awe • Step by Step • We Fall Down • You Are My King (Amazing Love) • and more.
00311024 Piano Solo..............$12.99

Blessings
THE PHILLIP KEVEREN SERIES
Phillip Keveren delivers another stellar collection of piano solo arrangements perfect for any reverent or worship setting: Blessed Be Your Name • Blessings • Cornerstone • Holy Spirit • This Is Amazing Grace • We Believe • Your Great Name • Your Name • and more.
00156601 Piano Solo $12.99

The Best Praise & Worship Songs Ever
80 all-time favorites: Awesome God • Breathe • Days of Elijah • Here I Am to Worship • I Could Sing of Your Love Forever • Open the Eyes of My Heart • Shout to the Lord • We Bow Down • dozens more.
00311057 P/V/G $22.99

The Big Book of Praise & Worship
Over 50 worship favorites are presented in this popular "Big Book" series collection. Includes: Always • Cornerstone • Forever Reign • I Will Follow • Jesus Paid It All • Lord, I Need You • Mighty to Save • Our God • Stronger • 10,000 Reasons (Bless the Lord) • This Is Amazing Grace • and more.
00140795 P/V/G $24.99

Contemporary Worship Duets
arr. Bill Wolaver
Contains 8 powerful songs carefully arranged by Bill Wolaver as duets for intermediate-level players: Agnus Dei • Be unto Your Name • He Is Exalted • Here I Am to Worship • I Will Rise • The Potter's Hand • Revelation Song • Your Name.
00290593 Piano Duets $10.99

51 Must-Have Modern Worship Hits
A great collection of 51 of today's most popular worship songs, including: Amazed • Better Is One Day • Everyday • Forever • God of Wonders • He Reigns • How Great Is Our God • Offering • Sing to the King • You Are Good • and more.
00311428 P/V/G $22.99

Hillsong Worship Favorites
12 powerful worship songs arranged for piano solo: At the Cross • Came to My Rescue • Desert Song • Forever Reign • Holy Spirit Rain Down • None but Jesus • The Potter's Hand • The Stand • Stronger • and more.
00312522 Piano Solo..................$12.99

The Best of Passion
Over 40 worship favorites featuring the talents of David Crowder, Matt Redman, Chris Tomlin, and others. Songs include: Always • Awakening • Blessed Be Your Name • Jesus Paid It All • My Heart Is Yours • Our God • 10,000 Reasons (Bless the Lord) • and more.
00101888 P/V/G $19.99

Praise & Worship Duets
THE PHILLIP KEVEREN SERIES
8 worshipful duets by Phillip Keveren: As the Deer • Awesome God • Give Thanks • Great Is the Lord • Lord, I Lift Your Name on High • Shout to the Lord • There Is a Redeemer • We Fall Down.
00311203 Piano Duet.................$12.99

Shout to the Lord!
THE PHILLIP KEVEREN SERIES
14 favorite praise songs, including: As the Deer • El Shaddai • Give Thanks • Great Is the Lord • How Beautiful • More Precious Than Silver • Oh Lord, You're Beautiful • A Shield About Me • Shine, Jesus, Shine • Shout to the Lord • Thy Word • and more.
00310699 Piano Solo $14.99

The Chris Tomlin Collection – 2nd Edition
15 songs from one of the leading artists and composers in Contemporary Christian music, including the favorites: Amazing Grace (My Chains Are Gone) • Holy Is the Lord • How Can I Keep from Singing • How Great Is Our God • Jesus Messiah • Our God • We Fall Down • and more.
00306951 P/V/G $17.99

Top Christian Downloads
21 of Christian music's top hits are presented in this collection of intermediate level piano solo arrangements. Includes: Forever Reign • How Great Is Our God • Mighty to Save • Praise You in This Storm • 10,000 Reasons (Bless the Lord) • Your Grace Is Enough • and more.
00125051 Piano Solo..................$14.99

Top Worship Downloads
20 of today's chart-topping Christian hits, including: Cornerstone • Forever Reign • Great I Am • Here for You • Lord, I Need You • My God • Never Once • One Thing Remains (Your Love Never Fails) • Your Great Name • and more.
00120870 P/V/G $16.99

The World's Greatest Praise Songs
Shawnee Press
This is a unique and useful collection of 50 of the very best praise titles of the last three decades. Includes: Above All • Forever • Here I Am to Worship • I Could Sing of Your Love Forever • Open the Eyes of My Heart • and so many more.
35022891 P/V/G $19.99

HAL•LEONARD®
www.halleonard.com
P/V/G = Piano/Vocal/Guitar Arrangements